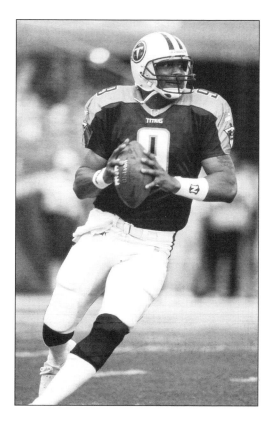

CREATIVE EDUCATION

TENNESSEE TITANS

JULIE NELSON

Published by Creative Education
123 South Broad Street, Mankato, Minnesota 56001
Creative Education is an imprint of The Creative Company

Designed by Rita Marshall

Photos by: Allsport USA, Bettmann/CORBIS, SportsChrome

Library of Congress Cataloging-in-Publication Data

Nelson, Julie.
Tennessee Titans / by Julie Nelson.
p. cm. — (NFL today)
Summary: A history of the professional football team that began in Houston and
was moved to Memphis in 1997.
ISBN 1-58341-062-7

1. Tennessee Titans (Football team)—Juvenile literature. [1. Tennessee
Titans (Football team)—History. 2. Football—History.] I. Title. II. Series: NFL
today (Mankato, Minn.)

GV956.T45N45   2000
796.332'64'0976819—dc21   99-015760

First edition

9 8 7 6 5 4 3 2 1

For years, many people have associated the state of Tennessee with country singers, cowboy hats, and guitars. Today, more and more people also picture footballs when thinking of Tennessee. On the collegiate level, the 1998 national champion University of Tennessee Volunteers are a football powerhouse. Professionally, the franchise formerly known as the Houston Oilers played its first season in Memphis, Tennessee, in 1997, and fans today anticipate years of gridiron thrills in Nashville's new Adelphia Coliseum.

Nashville is often referred to as the "Athens of the South," so it is only fitting that the city's new football team took its

One of the first Oilers stars, halfback Billy Cannon.

name from Greek mythology. According to mythology, the Titans were a race of giants who fought against the Greek gods. One Titan named Prometheus was said to have given mankind the gift of fire. The great size and power of the Titans made the name a popular choice when Tennessee chose a new name for its football team.

The Titans began their history in the late 1950s when the club's founder and owner, K.S. "Bud" Adams, sought permission to put a National Football League franchise in Houston, Texas, calling them the Oilers. When the league turned him down, however, he helped form the American Football League to compete against the NFL for players and fans. Ten years later, a successful Houston franchise finally joined the NFL when the two leagues merged into one.

For more than 35 years, the Oilers were known for their special brand of hard-driving and high-flying football. Today, the Titans of Tennessee plan to continue that legacy.

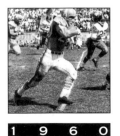

1 9 6 0

Billy Cannon led all Houston running backs with 644 yards.

STARTING OUT ON TOP

It is only natural that the history of the Houston Oilers is closely tied to the fortunes of a Texas oil man—Bud Adams. Adams lettered in football in both high school and college. World War II and success in the oil business deflected Adams away from a pro career, but he never lost his love for the sport. Adams was one of the first people fellow Texan Lamar Hunt contacted in 1959 about buying a team in the new AFL.

Nothing came easy for the Oilers at first, but almost everything turned out right. First, the team selected halfback Billy

Quarterback Steve "Air" McNair.

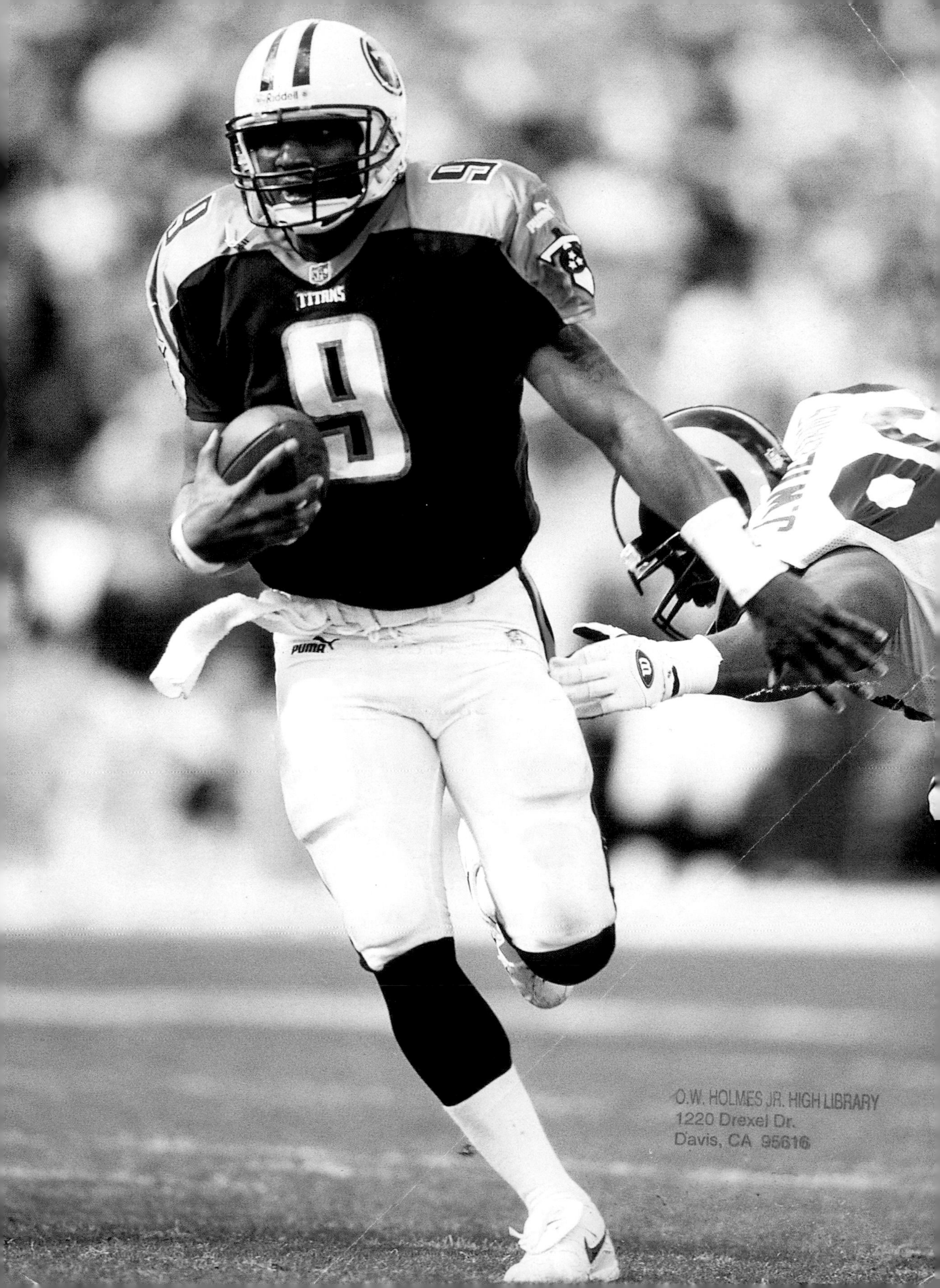
TITANS
PUMA

George Blanda set an AFL record by throwing seven touchdown passes in a single game.

Cannon, the Heisman Trophy winner from Louisiana State University, as its first college draft pick. Houston even signed him on the field of the Sugar Bowl on January 1, 1960. Then the NFL's Los Angeles Rams produced a similar contract signed by Cannon. The two teams went to court over the matter, and a judge ruled in Houston's favor. Cannon went on to star in Houston for four years.

A second bit of luck for the Oilers involved the signing of quarterback George Blanda before the 1960 season. Blanda, who was both a passer and a placekicker, had an up-and-down career with the Chicago Bears from 1949 to 1958. In 1959, after he was traded to the Baltimore Colts, he decided to retire. Oilers coach Lou Rymkus approached Blanda, however, and tried to convince the quarterback that someone with his competitive fire should be playing football every week—not watching it.

The challenge appealed to the 33-year-old Blanda, and he began a new career in the AFL that lasted until he was nearly 49. Blanda played in Houston for seven of those years, leading the Oilers to first-place finishes in the AFL's Eastern Division during the league's first three seasons and to league championships in both 1960 and 1961. After setting pro records for most seasons played (26), most games played (340), and most points scored (2,002) in a career, Blanda was inducted into the Pro Football Hall of Fame in 1981.

The Oilers' one major problem in their early years involved finding a suitable place to play home games. The only available site was Jeppesen Stadium, a local high school field, which the club renovated to seat up to 36,000 spectators. The shabby surroundings did not attract fans at first, but the team's outstanding play soon did. At the end of the 1960 season, more than 32,000 people packed into Jeppesen to watch the Oilers defeat the Los Angeles Chargers 31–23 to capture the first-ever AFL championship.

The following year, Adams helped to get an $18 million bond issue passed to finance the building of the Harris County Domed Stadium, better known as the Houston Astrodome. The Oilers would finally move into the "domed wonder" in 1968.

Cornerback Bobby Jancik used his speed to star as a kick returner.

While they waited for their new home to be finished, though, the Oilers stayed atop the AFL standings in both 1961 and 1962. In 1961, the team got off to a slow start before pulling off 10 wins in a row. Along the way, Houston became the first team in pro football history to score more than 500 points in a season. The Oilers ended the year with a narrow 10–3 victory over the Chargers for a second straight AFL title.

In 1962, Houston kept up its offensive attack, led by Blanda's passing to flanker Charley Hennigan. For the third consecutive year, the club reached the AFL championship game. This time, the Dallas Texans (soon to become the Kansas City Chiefs) found a way to stop them, but it took a field goal in double-overtime to end Houston's reign.

THE OILERS' ROLLER-COASTER RIDE

That loss to Dallas seemed to be an omen of bad things to come for the Oilers. Houston suffered its first losing season in 1963 and then began a strange roller-coaster ride up and down the standings over the next 11 years. During that period of time, the Oilers had seven losing seasons,

Dominant defensive end Ray Childress.

All-Pro wide receiver Drew Hill. 11

*All-Pro defensive
end Elvin Bethea
set a team record
with 14 sacks.*

three seasons ending in .500 records, and one glorious winning campaign in which they came within a game of reaching the Super Bowl. Why the Oilers performed so unevenly is hard to explain, especially since they had four of football's finest athletes during that time.

Defensive lineman Elvin Bethea joined the Oilers in 1968 and went on to play 16 seasons and 210 games with Houston—both club records. He was a fast and powerful pass rusher, leading the Oilers' defense in quarterback sacks six different seasons.

While Bethea terrorized opposing quarterbacks with his fierce rushes, linebacker George Webster and safety Ken Houston drove them crazy with outstanding pass coverage near the line of scrimmage and downfield. Both players joined the Oilers in 1967 and had an immediate impact, helping to turn a team that had finished last in 1966 into a division leader. The Oilers reached the AFL championship game in 1967 but could not overcome the powerful Oakland Raiders to advance to Super Bowl II.

Webster and Houston continued to star in the league long after their rookie seasons. Webster was later named to the All-Time AFL Team by a special selection committee. Houston, a Pro-Bowl player for an amazing 12 straight seasons, was inducted into the Pro Football Hall of Fame in 1986.

Another Oilers star during that period was tall, handsome quarterback Dan Pastorini, who had won the hearts of football fans during his playing days at Santa Clara College. Pastorini came to Houston as a number one draft pick in 1971. The Oilers didn't have much of an offensive line during his first few seasons in Houston, so he spent much of his time scrambling away from onrushing defensive linemen. By 1975, though, Pastorini was ready for big things, and so were Oilers fans.

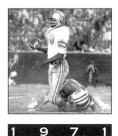

Safety Ken Houston returned four interceptions for touchdowns.

"BUM" AND "THE TYLER ROSE"

Despite fine individual performances by Bethea, Webster, Houston, and Pastorini, the Oilers lacked the leadership and guidance they needed to become a powerhouse. That would change with the promotion of defensive coordinator O.A. "Bum" Phillips to head coach before the 1975 season. During the next six years under Phillips, the Oilers would record five winning seasons, win two divisional crowns, and reach the AFC championship game twice. They would also

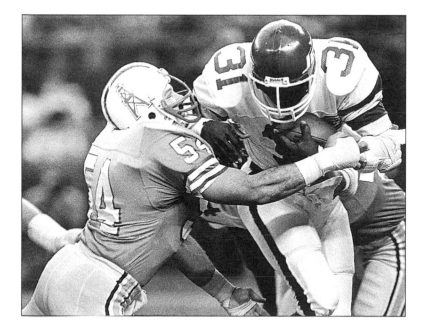

Hard-nosed linebacker Gregg Bingham.

Speedy receiver Billy "White Shoes" Johnson returned three punts for touchdowns.

pack the Astrodome week after week with rabid fans wearing the team's light blue and white colors and waving "Luv Ya Blue" banners.

It wasn't just his success as a football coach that endeared Phillips to Houston fans. His unique nickname and unusual style of dress on the sidelines—10-gallon Stetson hat, lizard or snakeskin boots, and a plaid Western shirt—also grabbed the public's attention.

Phillips began the rebuilding process right away in the 1975 NFL draft. With Houston's first three picks, he selected linebacker Robert Brazile of Jackson State, Texas A&I running back Don Hardeman, and Kansas wide receiver Emmett Edwards. He worked all three players immediately into Houston's starting lineup with positive results. Brazile, nicknamed "Dr. Doom" because of his hard tackles, was named an All-Pro in 1975 for the first of seven consecutive years. Hardeman became one of the team's leading rushers, and Edwards joined veteran receivers Ken Burrough and Billy "White Shoes" Johnson to form a great pass-catching trio.

Phillips's "new" Oilers started 6–1 in 1975 and finished with a 10–4 record, the team's first winning season since 1967. The big surprises for the year were Brazile's poise and leadership ability as a rookie, the Pastorini-to-Burrough passing combination that accounted for more than 1,000 yards and eight touchdowns, and the amazing play of Billy Johnson, who tied a league record by returning four kicks (three punts and one kickoff) for touchdowns.

Despite Phillips's initial success, it wasn't until 1978 that Houston really began climbing to the top of the league. The prize plum that Phillips plucked from the draft that year was

Haywood Jeffires followed Ken Burrough as a star wideout.

the incomparable Earl Campbell from [ ] Texas. In seven seasons in Houston, Ca[ ] four NFL rushing titles, set nearly every [ ] record, and be selected by his fellow NFL [ ] Thorpe Award recipient for Most Valuable [ ] secutive years (1978–80).

Campbell's outstanding play eventuall[ ] place in the Hall of Fame, yet his football p[ ] very bright during his childhood. "The Tyle[ ] name in college) had grown up in tiny [ ] tracted to pool halls and bars, he seen[ ] trouble. After he was shot in the leg during [ ] the young Campbell finally decided to buck[ ] all of his energy into football.

NFL fans got their first glimpse of Can[ ] during a nationally-televised Monday Nigh[ ] on November 20, 1978. In that game, Camp[ ] edly dismantled the favored Miami Dolph[ ] four touchdowns and 199 yards in a 35–30 [ ]

Campbell took command of games with a [ ] ture of power, speed, and determination. [ ] through people," Campbell explained. "A[ ] around them. I never said much as a player[ ] key, but I was really cocky on the inside. I [ ] was anything I couldn't do on a football [ ] more fun out there than anyone could imagi[ ]

Houston fans had lots of fun, too, cheerin[ ] talized Oilers. The Oilers reached the playoff[ ] first time in nine years. They came from bel[ ] Card game to defeat Miami again, 17–9, the[ ]

Earl Campbell bulldozed his way through defenses.

A longtime offensive fixture, lineman Bruce Matthew[ ]

England 31–14 to reach the AFC championship game against the Pittsburgh Steelers. There, a slippery, rain-soaked field and a smothering Pittsburgh defense did in the Oilers, 34–5.

The same two teams battled in the AFC championship game the next year as well—with the same result. Pittsburgh went on to win a second straight Super Bowl title, while the Oilers went home empty-handed once again.

Bum Phillips decided to pull out all the stops in 1980 in an effort to finally win it all. In a controversial trade, Phillips sent Pastorini to Oakland for veteran quarterback Ken "the Snake" Stabler. Stabler had Super Bowl experience, but he also had an aging arm and bad knees.

Still, the trade seemed to work out. Stabler passed for more than 3,200 yards—more than Pastorini ever had in one

1 9 7 9

Earl Campbell had a monster season, gaining 1,697 yards and scoring 19 touchdowns.

Guard Mike Munchak cleared running room for Campbell.

the incomparable Earl Campbell from the University of Texas. In seven seasons in Houston, Campbell would win four NFL rushing titles, set nearly every franchise running record, and be selected by his fellow NFL players as the Jim Thorpe Award recipient for Most Valuable Player three consecutive years (1978–80).

Campbell's outstanding play eventually earned him a place in the Hall of Fame, yet his football prospects were not very bright during his childhood. "The Tyler Rose" (his nickname in college) had grown up in tiny Tyler, Texas. Attracted to pool halls and bars, he seemed destined for trouble. After he was shot in the leg during a drunken brawl, the young Campbell finally decided to buckle down and put all of his energy into football.

NFL fans got their first glimpse of Campbell's greatness during a nationally-televised Monday Night Football game on November 20, 1978. In that game, Campbell single-handedly dismantled the favored Miami Dolphins, rushing for four touchdowns and 199 yards in a 35–30 Houston victory.

Campbell took command of games with an awesome mixture of power, speed, and determination. "I liked to run through people," Campbell explained. "Anybody can run around them. I never said much as a player. I was real low-key, but I was really cocky on the inside. I didn't think there was anything I couldn't do on a football field. And I had more fun out there than anyone could imagine."

Houston fans had lots of fun, too, cheering for their revitalized Oilers. The Oilers reached the playoffs in 1978 for the first time in nine years. They came from behind in the Wild Card game to defeat Miami again, 17–9, then crushed New

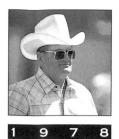

1 9 7 8

Head coach Bum Phillips led the Oilers to the AFC title game.

A longtime offensive fixture, lineman Bruce Matthews (pages 18-19).

Warren Moon made six Pro Bowl appearances.

year—and handed off to Campbell for nearly 2,000 more yards. The result was an 11–5 record and a third straight playoff berth. But the Oilers couldn't get past their playoff jinx. In a sad homecoming for Stabler, the Raiders trounced the Oilers 27–7 to end Houston's postseason.

As it turned out, Houston lost more than a game that day. In a post-game press conference, Bum Phillips admitted that his team had been "outplayed and outcoached" by Oakland. Upset about his coach's remarks, team owner Bud Adams fired Phillips two weeks later.

1 9 8 5

Former Oilers defensive coordinator Jerry Glanville took over as head coach.

GLANVILLE REBUILDS THE OILERS

Letting Phillips go proved to be one of Adams's worst decisions. Over the next four seasons, the Oilers went through three coaches and plummeted to a 2–14 record. The core of the team was changing. The offense was decimated by the departures of Stabler and Burrough in 1981 and by Earl Campbell's increasingly weak knees. The defense also began to suffer when Elvin Bethea retired in 1983 and Robert Brazile called it quits the following year.

Houston's decline was finally halted in 1985, when assistant coach Jerry Glanville took over as head coach. Glanville set his sights on returning Houston to the playoffs, but he knew that would take work. "When I came here in '84, we had the nicest guys in the NFL," Glanville later recalled. "But they couldn't hit if you handed them sticks." He wanted to turn the Astrodome into a "House of Pain," a place where visiting teams would feel the energy of the Oilers' high-powered offense and the force of their crushing defense.

21

Glanville's task of turning the Oilers into winners again was aided by quarterback Warren Moon, who had joined the Oilers in 1984. Moon, a former All-American at the University of Washington, had chosen to play in the Canadian Football League rather than the NFL after leaving college. He played six seasons with the Edmonton Eskimos, leading the club to the CFL's Grey Cup championship five straight years and establishing himself as the league's best passer.

With one of the strongest arms of all time, Moon revolutionized the Oilers' offensive attack for 10 seasons under coaches Jerry Glanville and Jack Pardee. By the time he left the Oilers after the 1993 season, Moon had established Houston records for career passing yardage (33,685), attempts (4,546), completions (2,632), and touchdowns (196). But he couldn't have set those records without such standout receivers as Drew Hill, Ernest Givins, and Haywood Jeffires. The amazing trio caught more than 1,500 passes during their years in Houston.

Glanville also focused on rebuilding the Oilers' defense. Drafting such players as defensive end Ray Childress and cornerbacks Richard Johnson and Cris Dishman, and trading for linemen William Fuller and Sean Jones, Glanville laid the foundation for his "House of Pain" squad. Houston fans loved their tough new team and began showing up at the Astrodome in record numbers.

Starting in 1987, the Oilers reached the playoffs seven straight seasons. But getting to the playoffs was one thing; getting to the Super Bowl was another. Houston lost in the second round in both 1987 and 1988. In 1989, a first-round overtime defeat to Pittsburgh ended Houston's year.

1 9 8 8

Mike Rozier powered his way to 10 touchdowns and more than 1,000 rushing yards.

Defensive end Ray Childress led Houston in sacks (13) for the fifth time.

That loss prompted Bud Adams to fire Glanville and turn the team over to former NFL linebacker Jack Pardee. Pardee decided to combine the club's best weapons—Warren Moon's speed and quick throwing release and the receiving abilities of Hill, Givins, Jeffires, and Curtis Duncan—to create a new kind of offensive attack: the "run-and-shoot." Most of the Oilers' new plays involved Moon scrambling out of the pocket formed by his offensive linemen and finding one of his receivers streaking across or down the field.

The results were remarkable. Moon completed 62 percent of his passes over the next two years for 9,379 yards and 56 touchdowns. Unfortunately, the Oilers continued to misfire in the playoffs, falling 41–14 to Cincinnati in the first round in 1990 and 26–24 to Denver in the second round in 1991.

Even those losses couldn't prepare Oilers fans for the bitterness that marked the end of the 1992 season. That year, Houston went into Buffalo's War Memorial Stadium as an underdog in the AFC Wild Card game but roared out to a 35–3 lead early in the third quarter. Moon couldn't seem to miss, and the defense, led by Ray Childress and safety Bubba McDowell, looked unbreakable. Then, the unthinkable happened. Combining touchdown passes from quarterback Frank Reich with daring onside kickoffs, Buffalo staged the greatest comeback in NFL history to take a 38–35 lead late in the fourth quarter.

Still, the Oilers weren't through. Moon rallied his troops for one more drive, which ended with an Al Del Greco field goal to tie the game with 12 seconds to go. In sudden-death overtime, Houston won the toss and took the opening kickoff. Moon threw an interception, however, and a face-mask penalty gave Buffalo the ball deep in Houston territory. Three plays later, the crushing defeat was sealed by a Bills field goal.

The Oilers rallied once more in 1993, winning their last 11 games of the season to post the best record in their history: 12–4. Yet the year ended the same as the previous six—with a playoff loss.

1 9 9 6

Quarterback Chris Chandler threw for 16 touchdowns in his second year as Houston's starter.

ON TO TENNESSEE

It seemed clear to most Oilers fans, and certainly to Bud Adams, that changes were needed. In 1994, Houston allowed Warren Moon to leave as a free agent. By mid-season, when the injury-riddled team was 1–9, Pardee was fired and replaced by assistant coach Jeff Fisher, who finished out a disappointing 2–14 campaign—one of the worst marks in team history. He then began to plan a major rebuilding effort.

The keys to Houston's overhaul project were two young stars selected in the first rounds of the 1995 and '96 drafts— Steve McNair, a quarterback from Alcorn State, and Eddie George, a Heisman Trophy-winning running back out of Ohio State. Although he had a great college career, McNair had never faced top-level competition at Alcorn State, and some football experts doubted his ability to become a big-time pro quarterback. Bud Adams had no such doubts.

"He's our most exciting draft choice since Earl Campbell," Adams said. "Drafting Earl turned our franchise around. Signing Warren Moon turned us around again. I see Steve McNair doing the same thing. You don't win a Super Bowl without a quarterback to lead the team, and I think Steve's the guy to do it."

Versatile tight end Frank Wycheck (pages 26-27).

25

*Safety Blaine
Bishop led all Oilers
defensive backs
with 82 tackles.*

In 1997, McNair, George, and the rest of the Oilers moved to Tennessee. Although the Oilers' 8–8 record in 1997 didn't exactly pack the bleachers with their new fans, the team didn't often disappoint those who came out to watch, going 6–2 at their home field in Memphis. George made his first season in Tennessee a memorable one, rushing for a whopping 1,399 yards.

1998 marked the Oilers' third straight 8–8 season. The team's offensive firepower continued to come from the one-two punch of McNair and George. McNair threw for 3,328 yards and 15 touchdowns, while George earned his second Pro-Bowl appearance by tearing through defenses for 1,604 total yards. On the opposite side of the ball, Tennessee was led by linebackers Joe Bowden and Barron Wortham.

Reliable receiver Yancy Thigpen.

Despite the solid individual performances, Tennessee struggled against the league's stronger teams. Following the season, Tennessee management brought in new talent in an effort to find playoff success once again. One of those players was University of Florida defensive end Jevon Kearse, the team's first-round pick in the 1999 NFL draft. Nicknamed "The Freak" because of his uncanny combination of size and speed, Kearse promised to immediately strengthen Tennessee's defense. "These kind of guys don't come along often with the athletic ability and play-making potential that he has," Coach Fisher said.

Kearse and his teammates would usher in a new era in a fabulous new stadium and wearing a different logo in 1999. Tennessee was finally ready to move into its 67,000-seat Adelphia Coliseum. But it would take that field as the Tennessee Titans, having changed its name and uniform. The team's new logo included the fire of the Titans, as well as three stars representing the state of Tennessee.

"I feel we have developed a logo that fans throughout the state of Tennessee and around the country will embrace for years to come," said owner Bud Adams. "It is a logo worthy of the nickname and of the brand of football I hope our team will play next year."

The Titans were a changed team in 1999, and not just in appearance. With a final record of 13–3, the Titans' rise to power was one of the year's most amazing sports stories. Another great story was that of Jevon Kearse, who used his incredible speed to collect an NFL rookie-record 14.5 sacks.

Tennessee's first opponent in the playoffs was Buffalo, and the Bills nearly closed the book on the Titans' story-

1 9 9 9

Linebacker Eddie Robinson led the Titans defense with 79 total stops.

One of the AFC's toughest rushers, Eddie George.

"The Freak," lightning-fast defensive end Jevon Kearse.   31

The Titans expected intense linebacker Randall Godfrey to make a big impact.

book season. After the Bills took a 16–15 lead with just three seconds left in the game, Tennessee pulled off one of the most amazing come-from-behind victories in playoff history. After fullback Lorenzo Neal caught Buffalo's kickoff, he handed off to Frank Wycheck, who lateralled the ball across the field to teammate Kevin Dyson. Dyson followed a wall of Titans blockers to the Bills' end zone for the winning touchdown as the stadium erupted in joy. "This will go down in history," Titans owner Bud Adams proclaimed. "There's never been another [finish] like it. . . ."

The Titans followed up the "Music City Miracle" by toppling the Indianapolis Colts and Jacksonville Jaguars to claim the AFC championship. The wins put the Titans in the Super Bowl against another underdog franchise: the explosive St. Louis Rams.

Although the Rams took a 16–0 lead, Eddie George led a Titans comeback that tied the score in the fourth quarter. After the Rams struck back with a long touchdown pass, the Titans put together one final, valiant drive. As time wound down, McNair completed nine straight passes to take his team deep into St. Louis territory. His final strike went to Kevin Dyson, who was brought down less than a yard from the end zone. "I thought we could do it, but we came up about six inches [short]," Coach Fisher said. "As much as this hurts, we have an awful lot of pride in coming so close."

After its amazing run to the Super Bowl, Tennessee plans to remain a dominant force in the AFC for a long time. With Kearse, McNair, and George leading the Titans ahead, soon the country music stars won't be the only ones in Tennessee with something to sing about.